R.E.A.P. More:
76 Seeds for This Season

Volume 1

Tammy C. Francis, Ph.D.

All rights reserved. No part of this publication may be reproduced, distributed, or transmitted in any form or by any means, including photocopying, recording, or other electronic or mechanical methods, without the prior written permission of the publisher, except in the case of brief quotations embodied in critical reviews and certain other noncommercial uses permitted by copyright law.

ISBN: 978-1-7355609-0-8

Catalyst 4 Change Global Publishing
Catalyst 4 Change Global
www.catalyst4changeglobal.net
DrTammy@catalyst4changeglobal.net

© 2020 All rights reserved.

Dedication

To Bridgette, my Sister, may my words help you on your journey. May they fuel your total restoration. May you find support and peace in the quotes and commentary to reap more and bring to harvest all you plant. You are amazing! I love you; I support you; and I appreciate the encouragement you give me. Thank you for continuing to fight. Thank you being my "ride or die."

To the Man who amazes me every day at his capacity to grow, learn, and give—to reap more. To Him who reminds me that what I do means something. To Him who serves as a teacher and catalyst for change in my life. To Him who encourages me and pushes me toward more. To Him who knows my heart despite my own censorship. Thank you for your open heart, protective gestures, and positive energy. Thank you for sharing your brilliance. Your excellence is inspiring. To Him. He knows.

Also by Dr. Tammy

Manifesting More: A Playbook for Planning and Living on Purpose

<u>*Chapters and Collaborations*</u>

Social Media as a 21st Century Playground
(in "Play in American Life" by Mary Ruth Moore and Constance Sabo-Risley, editors)

No Limit!
(in "Stronger: A Guide for Women Entrepreneurs on Finding Hope and Motivation for Business During Times of Crisis")

Flow
(in "You Can: 33 Stories to Uplift & Inspire Everyday People" compiled by Nina Motivates)

Introduction

I have always quoted other people and sought inspiration and encouragement from others. Then, as I was establishing a routine for posting on social media, I began posting daily and established Monday as a day to focus on motivation, quotes. The content on posts was original not shared or borrowed, so I decided to focus on original quotes.

Then, after realizing the encouragement I was giving others was also the encouragement I needed, I decided to compile these original quotes into a book for you, for us. I found myself going to my page reading my words to help me—to help me through and serve as a reminder, encouragement, when life becomes overwhelming or I lose focus. Why not compile them for others, for us? Why not make them into something that we can use during our time of reflection, meditation, or devotion?

So, I am offering 76 quotes with questions and reflective prompts to help us on our journey and apply to our life—to shift our mindset into a positive space ready to tackle the world and move in the direction of more.

I refer to the quotes as seeds because in all we do, every day, we have the opportunity to plant seeds that could grow into something we can use and/or help us on our journey toward more. We must plant them, water them, and give them light. Each seed (or quote) is designed to shift our mindset so we can allow love and positive energy to flow like water and light while we grow our goals into reality.

R.E.A.P. More

Learn. Move. Grow.

Teach. Travel. Transform.

1.
To create overflow, let it go!

We must create space for those things that are waiting for us. We must make room for our gift to grow. So, we must let go of those things that are no longer serving us.

What are you holding on to for dear life? What do you need to let go of to make room for more?

_____

_____

_____

_____

_____

_____

_____

_____

_____

_____

_____

_____

R.E.A.P. More

R.E.A.P. More

2.
The encouragement you give is oftentimes the encouragement you seek.

Listen to the messages you send out into the world! It may just be for you.

What messages are you sending out into the world? Time explore the self...

_____

_____

_____

_____

_____

_____

_____

_____

_____

_____

_____

R.E.A.P. More

3.
You can just GO through it or you can GROW through it. Choose.

When life gets challenging, it presents an opportunity to choose how you will make it through. Look to those challenging times as a growth opportunity. Hang on in there.

If you are going through, what are you choosing? Choose wisely.

_____

_____

_____

_____

_____

_____

_____

_____

_____

_____

R.E.A.P. More

4.
You vision and gift are designed and designated for you! Embrace them.

What you have been given, your vision and gift or talent, is made only for you. Only you can see your vision. Only you can use your gift or talent. So, embrace them. Pursue them. No comparing. No competing. Just do you!

What vision or gift are you ignoring? What are you refusing to pursue? Need a little clarity? Need support on your journey of discovery?

_____

_____

_____

_____

_____

_____

_____

_____

_____

R.E.A.P. More

5.
Think bigger than your BIG!

Your goals should stretch you! However, typically when we set goals, we set them in the safe zone. Your goals should be ones that push you, make you step out of your comfort zone, utilize untapped resources, ignite the creativity that lies dormant inside of you, create more ideas and more goals...

What are your goals for the next 3 months? Think bigger than that! How can you take them up a notch? What aspect of those goals could you adjust that would stretch you?

Reflect. Evaluate. Adjust. Plan. (accordingly) R.E.A.P. More!

Are you serious about moving in the direction of more? Do you want support on your journey?

_____

_____

_____

_____

_____

_____

R.E.A.P. More

6.
Don't procrastinate on someone else's breakthrough. Live your dream.

When we don't pursue our dreams or use our gift(s), we may be unconsciously withholding the very thing that another person needs to pursue theirs. It was given to you to serve others. If you ignore it, reject it, hide it, you are not using it or serving others with it. Do the right thing. Live your dream! Don't just pursue it! Live it!

Do you possess an idea that could bless someone else? Are you procrastinating? Do you need an ACTION plan? Accept. Plan. Execute.

_____

_____

_____

_____

_____

_____

_____

_____

R.E.A.P. More

7.
R.E.A.P. More!
Reflect
Evaluate
Adjust
Plan

To REAP More and receive the reward or the harvest of your labor, you must first put in the work, sow the right seeds. You must devote concentrated effort and action toward your goals and dreams.

Today, take some time to R.E.A.P. More by using this strategy to assess your goals for this week.

What seeds are you sowing this week? What will be your harvest?

_____

_____

_____

_____

_____

_____

_____

R.E.A.P. More

8.

Only put messages out into the world you would like to receive!

Recently, the words I share daily have been said to me. They have returned to sender.

What are you saying? What are sending out into world? What message will come back to you just when you need it?

_____

_____

_____

_____

_____

_____

_____

_____

_____

_____

R.E.A.P. More

9.

In life, sometimes we need to pause, just don't stop. There is power in a pause! Use it to reboot and recharge.

Storms, curve balls, situations, the unexpected, challenges, obstacles, whatever you choose to call it, happen; and sometimes, it knocks the very breath out of you. If there comes a time that you need to reboot and recharge, take it. PAUSE. BUT REMEMBER...

A pause is BRIEF and only temporary, don't stop—that's permanent, that's quitting... So, PAUSE. Use the time wisely. Keep working your *C4C Daily 3* (see the *Playbook* for the process and tools) and bounce back in beast mode...

Can't stop, won't stop!

_____

_____

_____

_____

_____

_____

_____

R.E.A.P. More

10.
If you want to do it, then you can do it. Harness your power!

Remember, everything you need is inside of you. So never question "if" you can do something; ask yourself "when" will you do it and just go for it. You got the power!

What are you putting off for better days? What are you ignoring, neglecting, or denying? You don't have to answer here. However, do share one task you will do this coming week that you have been putting off.

_____

_____

_____

_____

_____

_____

_____

_____

_____

R.E.A.P. More

ns the R.E.A.P. More

11.
Consider the possibilities!

What can you do today to improve your tomorrow? What are your options? What can you do to increase the probability you will get what you desire, achieve your goals, and redeem your dreams?

_____

_____

_____

_____

_____

_____

_____

_____

_____

_____

_____

_____

R.E.A.P. More

12.

Do what is in your soul!

What's in your soul? Do you know? What do you truly desire? Do that! Pursue that!

R.E.A.P. More

13.
Surrender to the moment.

When you are shifting or experiencing change,
1. Focus on the here and now.
2. Know you are about to go to the next level.
3. Stop resisting change.
4. Go with the flow. Create space for flow in the moment.

Trust the process. Allow the moment to guide you. Surrender. Surrender all.

How are you creating stability (at this moment in time)? How are you making your space secure? Are you ready and willing to grow? Are you ready for a fresh start?

_____

_____

_____

_____

_____

_____

_____

_____

_____

R.E.A.P. More

14.
Be EXTRAordinary!

I am EXTRA; I encourage you be EXTRA. So, let me elaborate. Each day, I wake up with the primary goal to be what extraordinary looks like. I aim to do those things that tap into that extraordinary part of Dr. Tammy, the aspects of me that make me unique. I encourage you to live authentically. I encourage you to tap into the EXTRAORDINARY part of you. Be extra!

How do you tap into the EXTRAORDINARY part of you each day? What are some ways you share who you really are inside? How do you share your magic?

Do it. And do it with excellence!

R.E.A.P. More

15.
Flow in peace.

Last night, I watched the 1993 movie, "Cool Runnings," which is a true story about the first Jamaican Bobsled Team that qualified for the 1988 Olympics. Yes, 30+ years ago. Anyway, in the movie, the team chose "Cool Runnings" for their name. "Cool Runnings" means go in peace, safe journey, and peace be the journey (urbandictionary.com). I began to think about my goals and what I want to work on next.

Since I am big on setting your intentions when working toward your goals, I encourage you to set the intention to FLOW IN PEACE! Find your "zone of genius" (*The Big Leap*, Hendricks, 2009), that creative flow. Create peace around that space. Flow in peace! Sometimes we must remove things or move things around to create peace, invite peace in. As you create or reassess your goals for this week, tap into that zone where you operate at your best and flow in peace.

How can you create peace? How can you create peace when you are in your creative space—physical or mental? What do you need to remove or move to create peace?

_____

_____

_____

R.E.A.P. More

16.

Patience is trusting the flow.

Patience gets a bad reputation. However, it shouldn't. Patience is not "moving" until you get confirmation from your inner voice or intuition. It's about taking a step back and regrouping. It's about timing. Patience is about trusting the process.

Are you trusting the flow in your situation? Are you trusting the process? Are you listening to your gut, your inner voice, your intuition? Where in your life or situation do you need to step back and regroup? How can you practice patience?

_____

_____

_____

_____

_____

_____

_____

_____

R.E.A.P. More

17.
Be the reflection you want to see.

Plain and simple. Don't do anything, don't say anything, don't be anything, you don't want done, said, or manifested. Govern yourself accordingly.

What are you reflecting? Who are you reflecting? What do you live?

R.E.A.P. More

18.
Let your light shine by living your truth.

In the 90s, we would ask each other as a greeting, "How ya livin'?" Today, I ask you the same question.

How are you living? Are you living the truth of who you really are? Are you letting your light shine?

R.E.A.P. More

19.

Cultivate your gifts and see the possibilities that dwell within you.

Have you planted seeds? Are you watering the seeds? Are you investing in your gift(s)? Are you allowing time to develop your gift(s)? What else is in you? What else has potential in you to grow?

Pause. Reflect. Write.

_____

_____

_____

_____

_____

_____

_____

_____

_____

_____

R.E.A.P. More

20.
Everything you have been through has led you to this moment. Be intentional.

You are exactly where you are meant to be at this point in your life. So, get into position! Accept the challenge! Where you are right now, it is with intention you are there...here. Now it's time for you to be intentional about the steps you take and decisions you make. Remain in a state of expectancy! Something amazing is about to happen. Don't sleep on it. Don't give up. Get ready. Be ready. Stay ready.

Have you reflected on where you are in your life? Have you taken time to evaluate your position? Have you mapped out your next steps? Have you reviewed your testimony? It's time to take action and share with others. You may just help someone else with your testimony and/or gift.

Get into position!

_____

_____

_____

_____

_____

R.E.A.P. More

21.
Flow with life.

Don't resist what comes your way. Don't run from what life presents to you. Just flow with it.

What are you resisting? What are you refusing to accept? What aspect of your life are you trying to change but nothing is happening? Reflect on these questions.

Below, share what you do to keep striving toward your goals, for more, despite the obstacles thrown your way. What do you do to stay motivated? What inspires you?

_____

_____

_____

_____

_____

_____

_____

_____

_____

R.E.A.P. More

22.
Birth what is inside of you. It is time.

Sometimes we get stuck in a place just waiting—not sure for what, but we are just waiting. It's time for us, yes, I said us, to birth what is inside of us. We often hear we are pregnant with purpose and possibility. It's true. Some of are walking around not fully releasing our gift and/or talents.

It's time! You feel it? Can't sleep? Can't think about anything else? Trouble focusing on the mundane? Something has your soul restless? Something has sparked your creative juices? Someone sees your potential, but it is uncomfortable because you're not ready to release? Those are called labor pains. It's time for you, us, to embrace the process. It's not easy or pain-free. However, the reward at the end is all worth it. It's time!

Does this sound familiar? Did you find yourself answering yes? Did you notice your temperature rise in your body? Did you skip over some of the questions because you were saying yes too often? It's time!

_____

_____

_____

_____

R.E.A.P. More

23.
Resistance is internal. Overcome resistance.

When you have a vision for what's next and direction for how to get there, but there's something holding you back; it is resistance. Resistance is procrastination, fear, self-doubt, and so much more. Resistance is internal. There's something inside of you that is holding you back, keeping you where you are, and stopping you from walking into your greatness. Resistance shows up over and over again. Resistance is an ongoing struggle. Therefore, we must acknowledge the resistance within and how it shows up for us; it is different for every person.

How does it look or show up for you? How does it feel in your body? What's keeping you from doing what you are meant to do? What's holding you back?

To answer these questions and be honest with yourself are the first steps in overcoming resistance. Pushing through your internal roadblock.

_____

_____

_____

_____

_____

_____

R.E.A.P. More

24.
Do what others won't do.

What are you willing to do to get what has your name on it?

Correct Answer: Anything! (Smile)

We should be willing to do what others won't do. We must be willing and ready to claim what's ours.

Now, we will not ignore strategy and timing, but we should be willing to be uncomfortable and step out of our comfort zone to get what has been designed and designated for us. Do what others won't do!

_____

_____

_____

_____

_____

_____

_____

_____

_____

_____

R.E.A.P. More

25.
Listen to the whispers.

Sometimes the messages we desire, the confirmation we seek, come in whispers. Sometimes it's not obvious. However, I do believe that we will hear more than one. We will hear whispers, not just a whisper. Therefore, we must listen. We must pay attention because if we ask, if we seek resolution, we will receive the direction, message, or confirmation we seek. But we must listen. This means we must get quiet and listen. Consistently, create space to receive.

When was the last time you took a moment to get quiet? Have you asked for direction, a message, and/or confirmation? Have you actually waited for the answer and listened to your heart? Have you surveyed your body for the emotional response? Listen carefully.

_____

_____

_____

_____

_____

_____

R.E.A.P. More

26.
Bend don't break.
(Be like a palm tree.)

This message kept coming to me over and over. Coincidence? I doubt it. So, I thought I'd share this with you too. Bend don't break. Be like a palm tree.

Palm trees are typically planted near the coast because of their durability. They are strong. They have deep roots and are flexible for climates more prone to extremely windy conditions. During a storm, they can bend and not break. We must be like the palm tree when life gets overwhelming or extremely challenging. Don't quit. Don't give up. Remain deeply rooted, grounded. Bend don't break.

Are you stretched thin? Are you at your wits end about something? Are you giving up or putting aside your goals and/or dreams to accommodate someone else or others? Are you always giving and not receiving? Bend don't break.

_____

_____

_____

_____

_____

R.E.A.P. More

27.
Impatience is a test of your commitment and dedication!

Will you wait for what is yours? What areas of your life and/or business is impatience showing up? When are you most impatient with yourself or others? Is it tied to something you are committed or dedicated to in your life or business?

Impatience may be a sign you're on the right track. Now, you just have to "fight the feeling" and wait. Be patient. In time, what you desire and what has been designated and designed for you will be yours. Pause. Listen. There is power in the pause. So, wait for the whispers.

_____

_____

_____

_____

_____

_____

_____

_____

R.E.A.P. More

28.

As you go higher, expect your circle to get smaller and your atmosphere to change.

You can't take dead weight with you as you go higher. When you are meant to do more, be more, you will notice your circle of influence, your circle of friends, will change. Don't be alarmed. Know that when you are called to do more, be great, the energy around you must also change. Your circle and atmosphere must align with where you are going. Expect it! Consider it a sign you're on the right track. Keep pressing. Keep pushing.

Have you notice some friends and even family who no longer bring the same energy when their around? Have you notice distance grow between you and certain people in your circle? Have you wondered recently why "so and so" has not been around lately? Have you noticed that when certain people are around or in your space the energy in your body is negative, tense? You may be witnessing the change I speak of here. Take note. Embrace what's next for you.

_____

_____

_____

_____

R.E.A.P. More

29.
Opposition does not mean you need to detour.

When you face opposition in your life, you are being prepared for greater. So, don't resist it. Don't go around it. If you are aspiring for more, expect it. Stay the course. Remember your vision. Think of the opposition as a test of how prepared you are and ready to claim what's yours. Face it head-on and claim what is yours.

2018 was a year of opposition and resistance for me. However, it is my testimony that if you stay the course, don't falter or waiver, continue do those things that are in alignment with who you are and your vision, there will be light at the end of the tunnel. Y'all, I even have more clarity; my vision for my life and business has never been clearer. I'm ready. Ready for OVERFLOW!

Are you experiencing opposition? What is your vision for your life or business? Are you taking a detour? Are you staying the course?

_____

_____

_____

_____

_____

_____

R.E.A.P. More

30.

Don't run from it; speak to it! Courage.

What are you avoiding? What are you refusing to do, have, say, or be?

Just face it head-on. Be courageous. Courage increases your confidence. Confidence allows you move in the direction of more without hesitation or self-doubt. Grow through it!

_____

_____

_____

_____

_____

_____

_____

_____

_____

_____

R.E.A.P. More

31.

Words can change things. Choose them wisely.

What you say and how you say it matters. Words can make a positive or negative impact on another person and on yourself. Positively speak. Delete words like "can't" and "try" from your vocabulary. What you speak, manifests!

What are you manifesting? How are you using words to get what you want? Choose your words wisely.

_____

_____

_____

_____

_____

_____

_____

_____

_____

R.E.A.P. More

32.
Raise your vibration.

Raise your vibration. We must tap into the power of intention. Become aware of our thoughts and feelings. Do things that puts us in a place of turning our dreams into reality. Manifesting!

What are some things you can do to connect to your thoughts or feelings? How do you raise your vibrations?

Here are a few ways to get you started:
1. Read a book. Stimulate your mind.
2. Create affirmations and repeat them.
3. Meditate. (morning and night)
4. Be intentional.
5. Surround yourself with positive people.

R.E.A.P. More

33.
Be good. Do good.

Be good. Do good. Then, all is good. That is all. What "good" are you sending out into the world? What "good" are you doing for yourself and/or others?

_____

_____

_____

_____

_____

_____

_____

_____

_____

_____

_____

R.E.A.P. More

34.

During transition, expect restlessness.

Wednesday, October 3, 2018 was one of the most difficult days of my life. My Granny, affectionately called by her grandchildren, was transitioning. While caring for her during that time, I witnessed the physical restlessness.

I began to think about the people, the Conscious Catalysts, I talk with daily either individually or in my groups. My platform is about creating cocoon experiences to provide a safe space for women and men to transition, change, become more self-aware, to be a better version of themselves. I have witnessed the restless soul— personally and in those who choose to level up. What I have realized, it's apart of the process. It's natural. It's okay. So, we must trust the process.

What change is happening in your life that is causing restlessness? What is pushing you to move out of your comfort zone? How are you dealing with that restlessness and discomfort?

_____

_____

_____

_____

_____

R.E.A.P. More

35.

As you grow, your atmosphere will change.

As you grow, your atmosphere will change. Your vision will evolve. Your circle will change. Your air will change. The very air you breathe will change. You will feel different. You will move different. You will interact with others different.

Being a catalyst for change and prompting a change in your atmosphere are my life's purpose, my life's work... The cocoon experiences I create and offer to those who choose to join my community, my tribe, are my way of precipitating change in the atmosphere for them, us—you and me.

_____

_____

_____

_____

_____

_____

_____

_____

_____

R.E.A.P. More

36.

If your crowd is getting smaller, you're getting closer to your destiny.

As you grow and change, you will notice a natural change in the crowd you hang with, your circle. As you transform into more and move in the direction of more, the friends and family you were once close to and talk to will change and/or get smaller. As you move toward what you are meant to do, be and have, your destiny, your circle will get smaller.

Is your crowd getting smaller? Is your circle getting smaller? Are you noticing a change in your atmosphere? You may be close!

_____

_____

_____

_____

_____

_____

_____

R.E.A.P. More

37.

Leave the room better than you found it.

Check your energy! Your energy should raise the vibration of any space you occupy. When you leave the room, it should better than you found it. Your energy should reflect positively on and in those you come in contact with daily.

If not, it's time to evaluate how you show up. How are you showing up each day? What value do you add to the spaces you occupy? How do you ensure that the energy you possess is the energy that others desire or need? How do you remain positive? How do you make others smile?

_____

_____

_____

_____

_____

_____

_____

_____

R.E.A.P. More

38.
During the silence of pivotal moments, you will hear the answers you seek.

This is encouragement for those going through. What you're going through is not easy nor clear; however, create a space for silence. Find time in your day for some quiet moments. Time to be in the presence of silence, with NO distraction or need to hurry. Just be.

As you create time for silence, you will find that the fog lifts on the road ahead. Silence is like a GPS for your journey. When you allow silence to dwell around you, all that is unknown becomes known. All that you question is answered. All the unsolved problems begin to have solutions.

During the silence, listen. Listen with an open heart.

Do you carve out time to be alone in the quiet? Do you have quiet time set aside during your day? Do you sit and journal? How do you capture the thoughts or ideas that come to you? Have you noticed when you get your best ideas? It's probably during the times when you are in silence or alone. Hmmm.

_____

_____

_____

_____

R.E.A.P. More

39.
Your past pushes you toward your purpose.

Most people want to forget certain aspects of their life. They want the past to be the past. However, I will beg to differ. Our life experiences are set up to propel us into our next. Our past is meant to push us toward our purpose. We must use what we learn to move us forward in everything. Use what we learn and go through as fuel to move us in the direction of more.

Rhetorical questions, just reflect on the answers and write here or in your *Playbook*. What experiences are you denying from your past? What experience(s) would you choose to forget? How can the experiences you'd like to forget serve as lessons learned for your NEXT? What is standing in your way of where you are and where you want to be? What is between what you have and what you desire?

_____

_____

_____

_____

_____

R.E.A.P. More

40.
Move in the direction of more and prepare for what's next.

What are you doing to prepare for what's next for you? What are your goals? What is one thing you'd like to accomplish or complete within the next 90 days? What does it look like, feel like, sound like when you do?

Like Big John McCarthy, the UFC referee, says, "You ready? You ready? Let's get it on!"

_____

_____

_____

_____

_____

_____

_____

_____

_____

_____

R.E.A.P. More

41.

Living on purpose requires purpose planning.

I designed the Playbook, *Manifesting More: A Playbook for Planning and Living on Purpose*, to help you do just that—live on purpose—to help you get what you desire. We must write down, with pen and paper, to know what it is we want and how to get it. We must visualize it. We must break it down into manageable tasks to reach our goals without becoming overwhelmed or frustrated. We must have an action plan that we can execute and adjust along the way. We must BE INTENTIONAL.

What are you wanting more of right now? What are your goals right now? What are you wanting more of next year? Where would you like to be next year? What will you be more intentional about right now, next week, next month, next quarter, next year?

_____

_____

_____

_____

_____

_____

_____

R.E.A.P. More

42.

If you cut corners, you'll only end up going in circles.

Sometimes we try to take the easy way out. Sometimes we try to get the hook up. Sometimes we even try to get a lot for a little. However, when we do that, we end just causing more heartache and headaches. We end up just spinning our wheels or following our tails. When we choose the easier way, we really choose the more difficult lesson.

So, as you are confronted with the decision to choose the easier way or not, what will you choose? Is it dependent on the situation? When was the last time you chose the easier route? What was the outcome? What lesson or lessons did you learn? Did you find yourself going in circles?

_____

_____

_____

_____

_____

_____

_____

R.E.A.P. More

43.

You can give back by making someone's today better than before your encounter with them.

We sometimes think it must be this grand gesture. It can be donating large amounts of your time, money, or gift. However, it doesn't. Sometimes we can make people's day just by offering a smile, opening a door, or giving them a compliment. Small acts of kindness can brighten someone's day. The same kindness that one day will find its way back to you just when you need it. How do you give back?

_____

_____

_____

_____

_____

_____

_____

_____

R.E.A.P. More

44.
When someone throws shade, shine sun back.

When someone is negative or unsupportive of your goals, your vision, always let the sun rays shine through! Let your light shine bright and pursue your purpose with passion. Don't let their shade stop you. Do you anyway!

How will you shine your light? What are your goals for sharing your gift or talent? How will you persevere despite what others say or do? How will the sun feel to you this year or next year?

_____

_____

_____

_____

_____

_____

_____

_____

_____

R.E.A.P. More

45.

If you are always in the shade, you never experience the sun.

As you set your intention for this year, this quarter, reflect on whether or not you are fully utilizing your gifts and talents.

Are you remaining in the background? Are you putting your dreams on hold? Are you dulling your shine because you're afraid of what others will say or do? Does the power you possess scare you?

It's time to walk into the sun. It's time to tap into your skills and abilities. It's time shine your light. Step into the sun! Absorb the creativity that will flow from the sun rays. Step into who you really are and meant to be.

Ready to dance in the sun?

_____

_____

_____

_____

_____

_____

R.E.A.P. More

46.
I surrender all—everything, all of it.

When your way doesn't work, then you must surrender all. For much of 2017 and all of 2018 and 2019, those 2+ years, were challenging. By living and growing through it, I have learned to surrender all when what I am doing is not working. It is on those days of overwhelm and frustration that I'm reminded.

Are you going through a shift? Are you going through one of life's storms? Is it time to let go? Is it time to trust the universe is conspiring in your favor? Is it time to surrender and follow the flow?

R.E.A.P. More

47.
Discover your bravery in the midst of your battle.

It is during the times when life hits the hardest that you discover your bravery. The courageous aspect of you comes to the surface. So even when life hits hard, remember to continue to reflect and take notice that the best of who you are is even more present than before.

How do you know Dr. Tammy? What I share each entry is my experience, a result of my experience. I encourage you to give yourself credit for your ability to keep pushing, for your strength, even in the midst of fear, danger, and/or difficulty.

Have you been brave this week? When was the last time you were courageous? What situation did you surprise yourself how well you handled it? Have you reflected and noted your courage in the midst of the storm?

_____

_____

_____

_____

_____

_____

R.E.A.P. More

48.

Don't allow your lips to violate your heart.

How important is it for those in your circle of influence to be moral and honest? When was the last time you made the choice to honor your word? Growing up, my parents and grandparents were big on "your word is your bond." A man's word means something and IS everything. It is also important that our words match our actions.

What is integrity? Why should we lead with integrity? Do your words match your action? Does what you say match what you do?

_____

_____

_____

_____

_____

_____

_____

_____

_____

R.E.A.P. More

49.

When the bar is too low, it's up to you to raise it!

Often, we settle for what is handed to us. In addition, we may even notice that the standards are low. Expectations are easy to fulfill. However, it up to us to acknowledge that the bar is too low for us, for our vision for our life, for what we aspire to accomplish, and RAISE IT. Set a new standard. Be a trendsetter. Create a new normal that continues to push the bar higher and higher. Never look to meet the minimum. Be the one that raises the standard and the expectations. Step out of your box and shine. Shine bright! Shine so bright that others around you are energized by your rays.

Have you raised the bar for yourself lately? When? How? Who has inspired you to strive for more, be more? Have you evaluated the expectations and goals you have set for yourself? Do they stretch you?

_____

_____

_____

_____

_____

_____

R.E.A.P. More

50.
Be expectant. Don't invite the energy of disbelief into your space.

Episode 10 of my podcast, "Journey Toward More," discussed how you can get what you want. I also share 5 things we need to do get what we want.

Being expectant is one way to manifest more of what you want. We must live as if what we want is already done. When we don't live that way, we are inviting the energy of the disbelief into our space. When you are skeptical, uncertainty dwells around you, your vision, your dreams, and your goals.

What are you inviting into your space? Are you confident what is for you is coming your way? Do you trust the process? Are you expectant?

_____

_____

_____

_____

_____

_____

R.E.A.P. More

51.
Honor your heart.

Our heart is special. Besides the obvious, the ability to keep us alive, our heart knows what we need, and it will tell us all we need to know. We just need to listen and honor it. So many times, we allow our mind to take over. Now, we should not ignore the mind and rational thinking. However, when we honor our heart, we tend to pursue our purpose with passion or choose the path that "feels right" to us. When we honor our heart, we also honor our gift. We honor what has been designed and designated for us.

What is your heart saying to you? What is your heart telling you that you need? What do you love to do? What are you passionate about?

_____

_____

_____

_____

_____

_____

_____

R.E.A.P. More

52.

Spark a reaction that precipitates change.

Create change. Allow each moment to inspire change in yourself or others. Each of those moment will spark a reaction and gain momentum. Those moments may also start a movement.

What are you doing to create change in the world? What are you doing to serve others and create change in others? How are you being a catalyst for change?

_____

_____

_____

_____

_____

_____

_____

_____

_____

R.E.A.P. More

53.
Decisions are the catalyst for turning our dreams in to reality.

When we refuse to make a decision, we cut ourselves off from other possibilities. Decisions create a space for focus and direction. Decisions teach us lessons and inform our next decision. Decisions create a learning environment—whether good or bad. Decisions can push us toward the next steps on our journey toward more. Decisions have power. Consider the power of a, just one, decision!

What decisions have you been putting off making or just plain avoiding? What is the one thing you will decide on today to help you move forward? What is holding you back? What are you afraid of? Is there a choice? Choose. Decide.

_____

_____

_____

_____

_____

_____

R.E.A.P. More

54.

Profess you are a winner; don't look defeated.

Do you look defeated? If you have to think about it, look in a mirror. Look into your eyes. Now, what's your answer? Do you know what a winner looks like? Do you know how you live as a winner and welcome winning into your space?

4 things to I want you to do:
1. Keep it moving. Pursue. Be proactive.
2. Set goals.
3. Focus on your goals. Put your "game face" on!
4. Smile. — Live. Laugh. Love.

You want people to ask, "Why are you so happy?" If you are claiming it, look like it! Act like it! Be a winner!

_____

_____

_____

_____

_____

_____

_____

_____

R.E.A.P. More

55.
Don't be imprisoned by your vision.

Dreams don't move toward us; therefore, we must move towards them. Stop waiting for the perfect conditions! Vision doesn't follow resources; resources follow the vision, your vision. If you don't pursue what you want and desire, it will continue to tug and pull at you. It will haunt you. You will stay stuck in the wilderness. Don't be held captive by your vision. Pursue it. Live it.

What is your vision? What is your vision for your life? Are you pursuing it? Is it nagging at you? Is it a cloud overhead? Are you trying to ignore what you are really meant to do? If so, how is that working for you?

_____

_____

_____

_____

_____

_____

_____

_____

R.E.A.P. More

56.

You have the capacity to recover.

Prepare for difficult times by building resilience to recover from life's challenges. It starts with your mindset. Remember, anything that comes your way and everything you have been through up until that point has prepared you for it. You have the capacity to recover. You are built to bounce back.

_____

_____

_____

_____

_____

_____

_____

_____

_____

R.E.A.P. More

57.
Cultivate the ground around the seed that has been planted inside of you.

To fulfill your dreams, you must cultivate the ground and nurture the seed. Your gift has been planted inside of you, so nurture it. Water it. Give it light.

Do something, despite how small, to help that area of your life grow and develop. Our gift is transformed by our experiences and what we do with it. Invest in your gift. Be consistent.

What is your gift? Are you nurturing it? What are you doing to grow and stretch?

_____

_____

_____

_____

_____

_____

_____

_____

_____

R.E.A.P. More

58.

Practice patience during the pause.

While waiting on your moment, you may feel like you're losing momentum. During times of transition and pauses, you must surrender to the process. Great things take time. Be patient with yourself and the process. Everything will be alright.

What are you waiting for? What are you wishing happened yesterday? What are you rushing to make happen? What are you discouraged about? What would you like to have happened, like yesterday?

_____

_____

_____

_____

_____

_____

_____

_____

_____

R.E.A.P. More

59.
Never negotiate your next!

If you know your gift, don't negotiate how you use and share it. If you know what's next for you, don't negotiate your "to do" list or the tasks you need to do to get there. You have been given your gift because it has been designed and designated for you. It is uniquely yours. No one else can do with it what you can. Lean all the way in. Go all the way. Don't stop. Don't change. Don't deny it. Don't delay how you serve.

NEVER NEGOTIATE your NEXT!!!

Have you changed your mind about what you'd like to do because it didn't suit someone else or their situation? Have you pulled back on how far or fast you use your gift or prepare for what's next because of others or their perception of it? Are you negotiating what you are doing or how you are doing it to accommodate others? Are you worried about how others perceive you or what you are doing to live on purpose?

_____

_____

_____

_____

R.E.A.P. More

60.
Challenges are the catalysts for changing our course toward more.

Sometimes we are faced with challenges that seem to knock the breath out of us. But even when you feel like your chest will cave in and your mind is overwhelmed, you must push through and gather the lessons along the way. There is something you need for your journey—collect it, acknowledge the lesson. Challenges are the catalysts for changing our course toward more. Hang in there.

What was a recent challenge you encountered? What did you learn from a recent challenge or obstacle? What's next for you? Which path is highlighted for you, and only you? What are you Manifesting More of this week?

_____

_____

_____

_____

_____

_____

_____

_____

R.E.A.P. More

61.
Detours redirect our path not the destination.

Detours are distractions. They are unpredictable and inconvenient. They throw us off track and make us feel like we don't know where we are going. They even extend our trip and require more time to get to where we are going. However, we must remember that no matter where the detours take us our destination is the same; our destiny is the same. When we allow ourselves to get flustered by detours, we lose focus and forget the original plan. However, if we would just read the signs along the way, they will guide us to where we are destined to be. Be confident in your pursuits. Be patient with yourself. Your destiny awaits!

What is distracting you from your purpose? Where have you been redirected? Is it taking you longer to get to where you want to be? Are you focused on the detour or destination? Are you focused on the distraction or your destiny?

_____

_____

_____

_____

R.E.A.P. More

62.

You can't manifest more making mediocre moves.

Manifesting requires a certain level of awareness—an awareness of yourself. It requires an awareness to walk, talk, and act as if it is already done. Therefore, you must:
♠ Be clear about what you want.
♠ WORK towards your goals.
♠ RECEIVE and acknowledge what comes your way and confirms you're on the right path.
♠ Get rid of any resistance.
♠ Trust the process.

Consequently, you must navigate the world, your space, with confidence. You must move about as if what you WANT is already done. The actions you take must align with your thoughts that are getting what you desire, want. So, you can NOT manifest more making mediocre moves. Your moves must be exceptional, optimal, number one, stellar, etc... So, grab your *Playbook* and start planning your next move. Let's go!

Are you happy with mediocrity? Are the tasks on your "to do" list optimal for reaching your goals? Are you showing up as your best self? Are you confident that what you want is heading your way? Are you navigating the world as if it's already done?

_____

_____

R.E.A.P. More

63.
Educators develop the powers within.

One of my greatest accomplishments has been doing what I love and enjoying it for 19+ years. Choosing education as a profession was the best decision I made as young 20 something. I am literally someone's teacher.

However, what I know is great teachers are game changers. Those teachers do not have to exist in a classroom or formal setting. We are all teachers. In living out our purpose with passion, we must not only serve but teach. We must share what we have learned on our journey with others. Our experiences and lessons empower others, give others fuel for their journey.

Who's your favorite teacher? Which teacher was most influential on you? How? Why? How do teach? How do you share what you know? How do you empower others with knowledge?

Teach. Empower. Transform.

_____

_____

_____

_____

_____

_____

R.E.A.P. More

64.
There is no power in possibilities and potential without progress.

We often consider the possibilities and acknowledge the potential of those things we like and don't want to give up-a relationship, job, outfit, car, etc... However, if we don't do what we planned or take ACTION on what we thought would take it (that thing) to the next level, then it is useless to us. It is not serving us in a way that adds value. It is not the best use of our time, money, or energy.... and let me just say/add this, our heart.

What are you holding onto because you believe it has potential? What are you holding onto because you believe there are possibilities? What are you holding onto that is taking your power? Are you giving your power away to something that is not the best use of your time, money, or energy? Are you giving your power away to someone who does not value your time, money, or energy?

_____

_____

_____

_____

R.E.A.P. More

65.
Flow in your gift.

Flow in your gift. To flow is to be in the zone. When you are operating in your zone of genius (Hendricks, 2009) and using your gift, you are energized, focused, and fully involved. You are enjoying the process. Synergy happens between your gift and your action. To flow in your gift makes an impact that changes yourself and others.

Do you know your gift? What do you enjoy? What are passionate about? What do you feel strongly about these days? What can you do for hours without thinking about it as a chore or labor? Are you using your gift? Are you sharing your gift with others?

_____

_____

_____

_____

_____

_____

_____

_____

R.E.A.P. More

66.
Stop waiting for what could or should be and start creating what will be.

STOP waiting for what could or should be and START creating what will be. That is all!

What are you waiting on? What are you creating? What are your top 3 tasks you'd like to complete this week? What ACTIONs will you take toward one of your goals this week?

_____

_____

_____

_____

_____

_____

_____

_____

_____

R.E.A.P. More

67.
Fighting failure forfeits focus on your future.

If you are fighting failure, your focus is not on your future. You're focused on the past and past experiences. Fail forward. Accept failure as detours, distractions, roadblocks, traffic jams, obstacles, etc... on our journey toward more. Use failure as fuel for the future. Keep your head up. Keep your eyes on your goals. Stay focused.

What are you focused on? Where are you devoting your energy? How do you feel about failure? What is your "failure-success" philosophy?

_____

_____

_____

_____

_____

_____

_____

_____

R.E.A.P. More

68.
Position yourself to persevere.

Do you feel like things are shifting? Do you need to adjust your strategy or plan? What sacrifice do you need to make to manifest more and get what you want? What will you do for freedom?

When things happen the way you plan or even go as plan, there still comes a time to reflect, evaluate, adjust and plan some more. R.E.A.P. More! We must do this periodically. We must take a moment to assess whether something that has come our way is opposition or an opportunity. We must assess whether something not happening or coming our way is a setback or a set up.

So, as you reflect and decide, make sure that whatever you are doing is getting you in position to persevere. Then, position yourself to persevere!

_____

_____

_____

_____

_____

_____

… More

69.
Be powered not pressured.

When are we pressured, we allow outside forces to persuade or coerce us into doing or being something. This life is way too short to allow others to dictate how we navigate the world, how we use our gift.

September 23rd is the birthday of my cousin who passed away at the age of 24 from complication associated with having Lupus. On the same day in 2019, I also found out one of major professors passed away. What I realized as I emotionally went through my day is that Pam encouraged what Dr. Griffith taught and preached. They both encouraged and inspired me to step out of the box, which is what I'm doing today as an Edupreneur—which fits me, my personality, my gift. Dare to be different and live life on your terms.

Be powered NOT pressured. To be powered is to be self-powered. To not need external power from no one or anything. To find your power from within and use it to impact others, to change the world. You can't serve if you are not powered from within, if you don't know what you possess within. Be powered not pressured.

What are you doing that is someone else's vision for your life? What are you believing that is someone else's belief? Do you know how much power you possess that can push you into your next? Have you looked within to reflect on if you are using all your power? Or are you being pressured, persuaded, or coerced into a position or path?

R.E.A.P. More

70.

When you are chosen, expect challenges.

Are you chosen? Are you destined for greatness? Have you been tasked with a specific purpose? Do you know what that is? Are you called or chosen?

Now, let me just say, many are called. Anyone can be called; anyone can answer the call. Anyone can say they can do this or that. BUT...

To be chosen means you are one of the chosen few. There are things that no one can do like you. It is your gift. It is your purpose. To be chosen means you are destined for greater things; there are plans at work that are bigger than you or what you can imagine.

To be chosen means you are selected and marked for favor. Therefore, expect challenges along the way. So, hang in there and PAUSE.

_____

_____

_____

_____

_____

_____

R.E.A.P. More

71.
Patience is trusting the flow.

Patience gets a bad reputation. However, it shouldn't. Patience is not "moving" until you get confirmation from your inner voice or intuition. It's about taking a step back and regrouping. It's about timing. Patience is about trusting the process.

Are you trusting the flow in your situation? Are you trusting the process? Are you listening to your gut, your inner voice, your intuition? Where in your life or situation do you need to step back and regroup or refocus? How can you practice patience?

This has been a huge part of my work as I started my businesses. Now, I'm ready. Let's go!

_____

_____

_____

_____

_____

_____

_____

R.E.A.P. More

72.

Your destiny partner is in rhythm with you.

One secret to fulfilling your destiny and making the journey toward your destiny destination is finding your purpose partner, your destiny partner.

Find your destiny partner. Your destiny partner does not disrupt your rhythm. Your destiny partner matches your energy. Your destiny partner is in rhythm with you. I have a theory behind fulfilling your destiny and living on purpose in purpose and this is one component.

Who is a part of your destiny? Who is meant to be a part of your journey? Who has been placed in your life to help you, push you, inspire you on your journey toward more? Who is raising your vibration and marching your energy?

_____

_____

_____

_____

_____

_____

_____

R.E.A.P. More

73.

Despite your scrapes and scares, you are special. So SHINE on!

As I have been talking with friends and family and reading about current events, I find it all to be a bit disheartening and sad. Folks are shrinking in the face of adversity and difference. We must realize that we may have bumps and bruises. We may have scrapes and scars. We may even have cuts and contusions. AND you can still be amazing. You are special. Your circumstances are not your conclusion. Shine your light! Shine on!

How are you shining your light? How are you using your scrapes and scars to share your story? What are your wins from last week? What are some of your recent successes?

_____

_____

_____

_____

_____

_____

R.E.A.P. More

74.
Bigger and bolder steps require inner work.

For 2+ years of my entrepreneurial journey, it was all about dreaming bigger, taking more risks, and living boldly—both daring and brave. I even did some things personally at the risk of messing things up and looking foolish. Although they were bold moves, I knew I had done the inner work the 2+ years necessary to embrace what's for me as well. Doing the inner work required to grow and prepare for what's next was not an easy task. It was looking at my reflection everyday and asking myself some tough questions.

Who am I, really? What am I really scared of? Am I holding on to something I need to let go of? If not now, then when? What matters most in my life? What am I doing about the things that matter most in my life? Have I done anything lately that's worth remembering? Have I made someone smile today? What have I given up on? When did I last push the boundaries of my comfort zone?

These are just some of the questions to start figuring out the work required. Look yourself squarely in the mirror and ask yourself and wait for an answer to come. It won't be easy at first. You may even laugh at yourself. But everyday show up for you! Remember: Bigger and bolder steps require more inner work, doing the hard part. If you keep pushing, you will find your power and maybe even uncover and discover your real purpose.

R.E.A.P. More

75.

Be gracious and kind while you shine.

Despite whom or what tries to dim your light, be gracious and kind while you shine. Things will happen unexpectedly to try to throw you off track, off your game. Hang in there. Don't give up. Don't quit. Keep doing what you're doing, especially if you know it is right or tied to your purpose. Don't allow others or other things be a distraction for what you are doing or where you are going. Stay focused. Stay the course.

What has been a distraction to you this week? What or who has disrupted your flow? What are you doing that is directly tied to your purpose? What are your goals to help keep you focused?

_____

_____

_____

_____

_____

_____

_____

R.E.A.P. More

76.
Greatness is in my DNA. Greater is the goal!

Sometimes I sit in reflection and marvel at my amazing ancestors. I am in awe at what they accomplished with so much working against them, so many against them. I have no doubt that GREATNESS is in my DNA. I could not do what I do without their sacrifice, BLOOD, sweat and tears. Therefore, each day, it is my goal to BE GREATER! Whatever I do great day, tomorrow, I must do and be greater.

People often ask me how I do what I do... All I can say is: GREATNESS is in my DNA. GREATER IS my GOAL! Mediocrity is not an option. Complacency is a disgrace. Settling is a shame.

How will you be greater tomorrow? What task(s) will you check off your "to do" list that will move you in the direction of more? How are you preparing for what's next?

_____

_____

_____

_____

_____

R.E.A.P. More

Afterword

We have just planted 76 seeds for this season. Next, we must water the seeds planted so we can R.E.A.P. the reward of this harvest. Hang on to this book and reread and reflect on what you have written and what you want. Clarify what is written based on new learning and positive mindset shifts along the way. Notice, this has turned into something greater, catalytic conversation between you and me, a journal, to provide instructions, directions, and fuel for your future, your journey. Take it with you. Use it as a guide or map for your journey, to manifest more. Harvest more. REAP more.

Plant. Reap. Harvest.

Share your journey of planting the 76 seeds with me. Let's start a global movement to plant 76 seeds we can sow and reap more.

#76Seeds #REAPmore #DrTammyFrancis

About the Author

Tammy C. Francis, Ph.D. is a native of Corpus Christi, Texas. Affectionately called Dr. Tammy, The Catalyst, she is an Edupreneur. She is owner and CEO of Catalyst 4 Change Global, LLC, Catalyst 4 Change Travel, T. F. Donaldson Global Enterprises, LLC, and Catalyst 4 Change Apparel. She is the founder of the growing Catalyst 4 Change Global Community. Dr. Tammy pursues all that allows space to teach and help others, so she does it all—well almost. She is a full-time tenured Assistant Professor who is also a Life and Business Strategist, Global Educator, Global Community Builder, Consultant, Educational Researcher, Literacy Advocate, International Speaker, Author, Podcaster, and Traveler.

As an entrepreneur, Dr. Tammy's passion is to help you discover yours, spark a reaction that precipitates change in your life or business. She chooses to educate, serve, and push others to aspire for more...more than their best. To embrace your greatness, one must explore the self; be self-aware. Therefore, more specifically, she helps those who are stuck move in the direction of MORE and prepare for what's next by providing them with the tools and strategies needed to plan and live on purpose in their life and/or business.

Her publication, *Manifesting More: A Playbook for Planning and Living on Purpose*, is the foundational tool to her message and movement. The Playbook is filled with life plays for this game called life and strategies to push you toward your passion with purpose. Dr. Tammy travels around the world offering Playbook Purpose Planning Parties—workshops, seminars, and retreats--to those who dare to aspire for more and move in the direction of more. She also shares with faculty and students how these strategies are beneficial to college students in nurturing student success behaviors.

As an educator, Dr. Tammy helps adults improve their reading and writing skills as well their ability to be successful in college and life. After leaving the secondary classrooms, she moved to higher education. She now teaches developmental reading and integrated reading and writing courses. In addition, Dr. Tammy occasionally teaches content area reading course for undergraduate and graduate education majors. Dr. Tammy also offers her services as a consultant and professional developer to assist faculty at the secondary and post-secondary levels with improving reading and writing instruction across the curriculum as well as sharing student success strategies and addressing equity and access in the classroom and within our institutions or organizations.

R.E.A.P. More

To connect with Dr. Tammy and/or participate in a transformational experience, you can join one of many opportunities she has for you to engage in the cocoon experience or follow her across all social media platforms @DrTammyFrancis. You can follow her community @C4CGlobal1 or www.catalyst4changeglobal.net.

DrTammyFrancis.com

Email: info@drtammyfrancis.com

www.linktr.ee/DrTammyFrancis

R.E.A.P. More

R.E.A.P. More

R.E.A.P. More

R.E.A.P. More

www.ingramcontent.com/pod-product-compliance
Lightning Source LLC
Chambersburg PA
CBHW020441110526
44587CB00037B/413